Truly Foul & Cheesy™

Genius
Facts
& Jokes

Published in Great Britain in MMXVIII by
Book House, an imprint of
The Salariya Book Company Ltd
25 Marlborough Place, Brighton BN1 1UB
www.salariya.com

ISBN: 978-1-912233-00-7

SALARIYA

1 3 5 7 9 8 6 4 2

A CIP catalogue record for this book is available
from the British Library.

Printed and bound in China.
Printed on paper from sustainable sources.

Created and designed by
David Salariya.

Visit
www.salariya.com
for our online catalogue and
free fun stuff.

PAPER FROM
SUSTAINABLE
FORESTS

Author:
John Townsend worked as a
secondary school teacher before
becoming a full-time writer.
He specialises in illuminating and
humorous information books for
all ages.

Artist:
David Antram studied at
Eastbourne College of Art and then
worked in advertising for 15 years
before becoming a full-time artist.
He has illustrated many children's
non-fiction books.

Truly Foul & Cheesy™

Genius Facts

& Jokes

This Truly Foul & Cheesy
book belongs to:

....

Written by

John Townsend

Illustrated by

David Antram

BOOK HOUSE
a SALARIYA imprint

Introduction

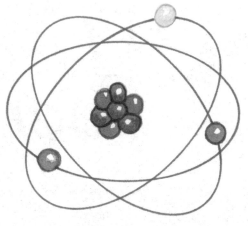

Warning – reading this book might not make you LOL (laugh out loud) but it could make you GOL (groan out loud), feel sick out loud or SEL (scream even louder). If you are reading this in a library by a SILENCE sign... get ready to be thrown out!

Disclaimer: The author really hasn't made anything up in this book (apart from some daft limericks and jokes). He checked out the foul facts as best he could and even double-checked the fouler bits to make sure - so please don't get too upset if you find out something different or meet a total genius, a boffin or a world expert on all things mind-boggling, who happens to know better.

I've discovered a genius gene... Oh no, it's just a very clever speck of dust.

Official

warning

This book contains some strange stuff about amazing people and their wow ideas. Being a genius isn't so much about having brain superpowers, but having the ability to 'think outside the box' and do something exceptional. Although a genius is usually thought to be extra clever, there's a difference between being really smart and being a genius. While geniuses can be mega-intelligent, they most often use imagination and creativity to invent, discover or create something new or special. You can't always spot a genius (there might be one very near you right now). If you happen to meet someone who is exceptionally intelligent, ingenious, brilliant, heroic, creative, eccentric, inventive, talented, bizarre or seemingly crazy at times, they could well be a genius. There again, they could just be stark raving bonkers. Be prepared to be surprised…

Genius limerick

If you think you've a
genius mind,
Don't smugly sit on
your behind
By taking life lazily...
Instead, take it crazily!
Some geniuses are
bonkers-inclined.

3

Quick genius quotes

'No great mind has ever existed without a touch of madness.'
Aristotle (philosopher in Ancient Greece)

'Genius is one per cent inspiration, ninety-nine per cent perspiration.'
Thomas Edison (inventor)

'Any fool can make something complicated. It takes a genius to make it simple.'
Woody Guthrie (musician)

3

Quick genius jokes

Did you hear about the genius duck being so eccentric that it just didn't fit in with all the other ducks on the pond? It was completely malardjusted.

Did you hear about the mathematical genius who's afraid of negative numbers?
He'll stop at nothing to avoid them.

Which animal is the genius of them all?
The donkey. Not only is it outstanding in its field – but it has the greatest brayin' power.

The genius of invention

Where would we be without the great inventions from history and the genius minds behind them? Just ask your friends what or who they think the most important invention or inventor ever was, and you'll get a whole range of weird and wonderful answers. We all have our own ideas about the most useful and important things in life.

So, let's start at the **BOTTOM**. Who was the genius **BEHIND** the toilet?
(You can't expect a book about foul facts and cheesy jokes to avoid such questions).
After all, the invention of flushing toilets, plumbing, sewage treatment and the supply of clean water has made a huge impact on world health and hygiene. That said, maybe 2.5 billion people around the world still live without proper sanitation.

So where did the genius of modern toilets begin? Did a caveman squatting over a hole in the middle of the night suddenly think, 'I'm going to invent an en-suite'? At first it was a potty idea...

I think I'll invent a luxury powder room.

Genius toilets

Ever since the first humans crossed their legs with an urgent need 'to go', people have come up with all sorts of creative ways to solve the problem of 'where to go'.

• Ancient Rome was famous for its public bathhouses – some serving 1,600 people at once for washing and communal lavatories. The city's mass toilets, with their long, benchlike seats, were not used by everyone, as many Romans just threw their poo onto the streets.

• Medieval English castles at least had a private room called a garderobe – a hole for royalty to do their business. The garderobe was usually suspended over a moat that collected all manner of human yuck.

• Peasants didn't have such luxury and often relieved themselves in the streets or directly into the river. No wonder rats and disease spread far and wide.

• Some rich people tried to improve matters. France's Louis XI hid his toilet bowl behind curtains and used herbs to keep his bathroom scented. England's Elizabeth I covered her commode in crimson velvet and lace. Even so, she still had to get her posh potty emptied.

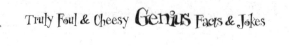

The Royal Flush

In 1596, Sir John Harrington, godson of Elizabeth I, came up with the bright idea for a new kind of water closet: a raised cistern with a small pipe down which water ran when released by a valve. The Queen installed Harrington's invention in her palace at Richmond, but it took another 200 years before a man named Alexander Cummings developed the S-shaped pipe underneath the basin to keep out foul smells.

There's definitely a whiff of genius about you.

Talking of foul pongs… some say a man called Joseph Bazalgette was a genius. He certainly changed London for the better. In 1853 – 1854, over **10,000** Londoners were killed by the disease cholera, carried in filthy water. It was thought cholera was caused by foul air. The hot summer of 1858 created the 'Great Stink of London', which grossed-out anyone who went near the River Thames (like one great open sewer). This is where Joseph Bazalgette stepped in – but not literally! He designed a new sewer system for the city to make sure the flow of foul water from old sewers and underground rivers was diverted along hidden channels, to new treatment works. Result = stink-free London.

In the 1880s, England's Prince Edward (later King Edward VII) hired a plumber named Thomas Crapper (stop sniggering) to construct smart lavatories in several royal palaces. Toilets were no longer just bog standard.

Toilet technology really took off in the 20th century, with flushable valves, water tanks over the bowl and even toilet-paper rolls. Today these seem like necessities, even though 40 percent of the world's population still don't have access to proper sanitation.

Another Victorian brainwave

Isambard Kingdom Brunel (1806–1859) was a genius of the 'heroic age of engineering'. Just as well. When entertaining his children with conjuring tricks in 1843, he accidentally swallowed a half-sovereign, which lodged in his windpipe. Mid-choke, the practically-minded problem-solving genius quickly knocked up a board pivoted between two uprights, strapped himself in, spun rapidly head over heels – and the coin flew out from the centrifugal force.

Isambard's other, more famous revolutionary engineering designs would change the face of railways, ships, bridges and much more. With a name like his, he could hardly be anything but extraordinary!

(By the way, it wasn't him who started the old cheesy joke about a man who swallowed a coin and was rushed to the doctor who waited patiently for the coin to come out the other end – with the announcement, 'still no change.' (No change – coin – get it?)

SIX

Cheesy inventor jokes

What did the genius say who invented the best way to make a cheese omelette?
'I know it's cheesy and eggstra-ordinary, but my method is **GRATER** than anyone else's.'

This is cheesier than a cheddar factory.

The inventor of the throat lozenge died last week. There was no coffin at the funeral.

The genius inventor of predictive text has sadly died.
His funny will be help on Saturn.

Did you know the genius inventor of the door knocker was awarded the No Bell Prize?
His wife invented the silent door knocker and was awarded the No Bell Peace Prize.
(In fact, the Nobel Prize is named after the Swedish chemist Alfred Nobel, who invented dynamite in 1867. His invention was bang on time!)

Did you hear about the French genius who invented sandals? He gave his name to beach footwear everywhere. Thank you, Philippe Philoppe!

The genius compiler of the most difficult crossword puzzles has died. He was buried in a ----- four down and six across.

This is even too cheesy for me!

Weird, wacky and wonderful

Many inventors have genius ideas but two rival geniuses changed the world with all their amazing inventions. Thomas Edison (1847–1931) and Nikola Tesla (1856–1943) both worked in the United States on all kinds of mind-boggling projects. Apart from being great scientists, both men could be quite eccentric.

When he was a child, Edison had scarlet fever, which left him deaf. Teachers told him that he was 'too stupid to learn anything' so his mother taught him at home, where he also had his own laboratory. He once made a friend swallow laxative powders which fizzed when mixed with water – in the hope the bubbles would make the boy float in the air. Instead, they had quite another effect!

When Edison started work, he was fired from two jobs but he didn't give up experimenting. He made 1,000 unsuccessful attempts at inventing the light bulb. All those unsuccessful attempts finally resulted in the design that worked and he once said, 'I haven't failed – I've just found 10,000 ways that don't work.' In fact, he was so busy inventing that he almost forgot his own wedding and had to be dragged by his bride to the ceremony.

Among Edison's
IMPORTANT
inventions:

1 Phonograph (recording equipment)

2 Durable light bulb (40 hours)

3 Electrical Vote Recorder

4 Telegraph

5   Carbon microphone

6   Electricity distribution system

7   First commercial fluoroscope (for X-Ray examinations)

Say 'Foul and cheeeeeesy'!

8

Cinematograph (motion picture camera)

Edison would sleep for four hours only in a day and would work for 72 hours at a stretch, especially when an experiment was about to be completed. He was still inventing when he was 80 years old, having already made over 1000 inventions.

Foul alert...

When Thomas died, Henry Ford (founder of the Ford motor company) creepily arranged for Edison's last breath to be caught in a test tube and preserved. That's just freaky!

'To invent, you need a good imagination and a pile of junk.' (Thomas Edison).

Nikola Tesla once worked for Edison and the two of them, like their electricity, often sparked! Tesla was a brilliant and eccentric genius whose inventions have enabled all kinds of modern-day power and mass communication systems that we can't do without.

The two sparking geniuses waged a 'War of Currents' in the 1880s over whose electrical system would power the world – Tesla's alternating-current (AC) system or Edison's rival direct-current (DC) electric power.

Tesla had an amazing photographic memory. He was known to memorise books and images, stockpiling visions for inventions in his head. He also had a powerful imagination and the ability to visualise in three dimensions, as well as speak many languages. He developed fluorescent lighting, X-ray machines, radios, televisions, and even the technology now used in smartphones.

BUT HE DID HAVE AN ODD SIDE.

- He had to wash his hands every few minutes and hated the sight of fruit, pearls or any round objects.

- He would only stay in hotel rooms with numbers divisible by three and always walked round a building three times before going inside.

- He freaked out if he touched human hair but loved pigeons (keeping them in his New York hotel room).

Most of Tesla's inventions really came up to scratch.

'The scientists of today think deeply instead of clearly. One must be sane to think clearly, but one can think deeply and be quite insane.'
(Nikola Tesla)

Newsflash

The inventor of the TV remote control disappeared last week. Eventually he was found down the back of the sofa but it was too late. There was no sign of life – even after the paramedics tried turning his batteries around and smacked him against the coffee table.

Genius inventions

All through history clever people have seen a need and got busy to come up with an answer. They say 'necessity is the mother of invention' but very often a mother is the mother of invention! Yes, shock... horror... many brilliant inventors have been women.

Here are 10 Women Inventors who made life better (with a foul fact hiding in the list)

1 Maybe you've never thought about it – but shopping bags with square bottoms are stronger and able to hold more than flat paper bags. In 1871 Margaret Knight came up with the design of a genius machine that could make square-bottomed bags. Even though a rival tried to steal her invention (claiming it couldn't possibly have been invented by a girl), Margaret gained a patent for it. Apparently, when she was 12 years old, she invented a safety device for cotton mills and became known as America's most famous 19th-century woman inventor.

I wish someone would invent a drinking straw for rats.

2 The inventor of the first ever car is a matter of debate but certainly a key inventor was Karl Benz from Germany in 1885. It took a few more years before an American called Margaret Wilcox invented the first car heater, which directed air from over the engine to warm the chilly toes of those early motorists. A touch of genius, Margaret.

3 How we all love injections. At least they're over quickly with modern hypodermic needles. Over 200 years ago, a sharp piece of glass or metal would be used to scratch open an arm to get substances into the body. Ouch! In 1853 Alexander Wood developed a medical hypodermic syringe with a needle fine enough to pierce the skin. But it took two hands to operate, so in 1899 Letitia Mumford Geer of New York designed a syringe that could be used with one hand (allowing the doctor to use the other hand for mopping up blood!). Remember Letitia the next time your doctor injects you with only one hand, while phoning for a pizza (or an undertaker) with the other.

I hope this injection isn't IN VEIN.

4 It took a woman in 1903 to come up with a solution to car windscreens covered in rain and snow. Mary Anderson saw how drivers in New York had to open their car windows to see out in the rain. So she invented a swinging arm with a rubber blade that was operated by the driver using a lever inside the car. It was also a woman inventor who first patented the automatic windshield wiper in 1917 (Charlotte Bridgwood's 'Storm Windshield Cleaner'). Monkeys in safari parks love them!

Instead of the car's wiper, I grabbed a snake.

It must be a wind-chilled viper.

If you are a fan of 'chocolate chip cookies', you have Ruth Wakefield to thank. In 1930, she was mixing ingredients at her roadside inn when she ran out of cocoa powder, so she added bits of broken chocolate into the mix, expecting them to melt into the dough and make chocolate cookies. That didn't happen, and the result made Ruth Wakefield a famous American inventor. The chocolate chip cookie became the most popular cookie in America and still remains so. Genius or happy accident?

 You may think solar panels to power homes are a recent invention. Over 70 years ago, Maria Telkes developed the first home heated from solar power. She was known as the 'Sun Queen', and worked on using the sun's energy long before today's world of solar heated homes and solar run cars.

7 Grace Murray Hopper was a computer scientist who invented important software programmes in 1959. Not only did she play a major part in developing computers, but she was also the first person to use the term 'bug' to describe a glitch in a computer system, after finding an actual moth causing trouble in her computer!

Stop bugging me!

Stephanie Kwolek was a chemist in the US, when she invented the stronger-than-steel fibre called Kevlar in 1965. Being five times stronger than steel, her fibre has been used to make bulletproof vests as well as having 200 other uses.

 In 1969, there was no such thing as CCTV. It took Marie Van Brittan Brown's system for closed-circuit television security, to help New York police respond quickly to crime. Her smart invention led to CCTV systems used for home security and police work today. Criminals caught on camera have genius Marie to thank!

10 In 1973 Shirley Jackson was the second African American woman in the United States to earn a doctorate in physics. Her amazing scientific research helped others invent such devices as the portable fax, touch tone telephone, solar cells, fibre-optic cables, and the technology behind caller ID. That's genius, surely, Shirley.

3 more
Cheesy jokes

What did the buffalo say when her genius son went off to university?
Bison. (Bye, son!)

When I was young, I reckoned I was a history genius and wanted to study archaeology, but my dad thought it was nothing more than a lot of skulduggery... though it's more like skull-diggery!

Q: Who are the smartest geniuses in the army?
A: Private Education, General Knowledge & Major Brainbox.
   (The daftest is General Ignorance.)

Whiz Kids

Some geniuses are super-clever from an early age. A few child prodigies were famous for being little smarty pants (but they must have been really annoying!) Meet three whiz kids who made their mark on history...

Blaise Pascal (1623–1662)

was a French mathematician, physicist, and philosopher. Even as a child he was a super-whiz. He wrote a scientific paper on vibrating bodies at the age of nine; he wrote formulas on a wall with a piece of coal at the age of eleven, secretly inventing his own terminology. He'd written a major theorem by the age of 16 and by 19 he had designed and built a mechanical calculator known as the 'Pascaline'. He died two months after his 39th birthday and once wrote in a letter: I have made this letter longer than usual because I lack the time to make it shorter. That's clever!

Wolfgang Amadeus Mozart

(1756 – 1791) was an Austrian 'wunderkind' and was practically born writing music. He played the harpsichord when he was just three years old and composed his first piece of published music at the age of five. Yes, he lived in a musical family but by his teen years, little Wolfie (as he was called) had already written several concertos, sonatas, operas and symphonies.

Wolfgang and his sister Maria Anna – herself a musical prodigy – travelled around Europe as celebrities. Mind you, Wolfie was a bit of a show-off. He would often play the piano blindfolded, make up tunes on the spot and could hear a complicated piece of music for the first time, then play it with no mistakes. Even at eight years old, he could sight-read music he'd never seen before. He could also be a naughty little chap, with a foul mouth. He made up nicknames for people such as Princess Dunghill, Prince Potbelly and Duchess Smackbottom. He easily got bored and that's when he acted like a cat by leaping over tables and chairs while meowing. He was also well known for being disgusting, telling toilet jokes and making up rude songs. How he'd like this book!

Mozart grew up to become one of Europe's most amazing composers. Before his death at the age of just 35, he'd written more than 600 pieces of music. That's genius!

I've no idea what I'm playing - 'no eye, dear', get it?

Clara Schumann (1819–1896) was a German musician who didn't speak until she was four years old but by the time she was seven, she was already spending up to three hours a day playing the piano. She began composing her own pieces at ten, and made concert performances in 1830 at the age of eleven. Clara then went on concert tours of Europe, where she astonished audiences with her ability to play everything from memory.

My memory is rubbish - I'm always losing it.

Clara married the composer Robert Schumann in 1840, but continued performing concerts and writing music when raising eight children. Sadly, her husband died and so did four of her children. By the time she died in 1896, Clara Schumann had spent six decades as a professional musician and played more than 1,300 public concerts. That's phenomenal!

Well I can't find it in here.

MAD

music joke

When Mozart died, he was buried in a churchyard and shortly afterwards the gravedigger heard strange noises coming from the area where Mozart was buried. Terrified, he ran to fetch the mayor, who placed his ear close to the grave. He, too, heard strange music coming from the ground.

Alarmed, he ran to get the town magistrate, who arrived and breathlessly put his ear to the grave. 'Ah, yes,' he said, 'That's Mozart's Ninth Symphony, being played backwards.' He listened some more. 'There's the Eighth Symphony, and it's backwards, too.' The magistrate kept listening; 'There's the Seventh...the Sixth...the Fifth...'

Suddenly he realised what was happening so he stood up and announced to the crowd gathering in the cemetery. 'My fellow citizens, there's nothing to worry about. It's just Mozart decomposing.'

Did you know?

Apparently, listening to Mozart in the cot could make babies brainy. Studies have suggested that listening to Mozart could raise IQ scores. Now parents have started playing Mozart to babies, hoping for the 'Mozart effect'. One explanation is that music makes people more awake and alert. Another is that listening to Mozart and mathematical tasks rely on the same neurons within the brain. It seems many a musical genius is also a whiz at maths.

After listening to Mozart in the bath I feel like a drowned rat.

Geniuses who had it tough

(late developers)

Like Thomas Edison, not all geniuses were good at school. Some people only achieved great things later in life after years of hard work. Some people's genius was only realised after their death.

Socrates (470 BC – 399 BC) was famous for being a great philosopher and the 'Father of Western thought'. He proclaimed himself not to be wise, but he was probably wiser than he thought! He came from humble beginnings but became a mentor to Alexander the Great. Despite leaving no written records behind, Socrates is regarded as one of the greatest philosophers of ancient Greece. Because of his new ideas, in his own time he was called 'an immoral corrupter of youth' and was sentenced to death. Socrates was claimed to say, 'I cannot teach anybody anything, I can only make them think.' He was instructed to drink poison as his punishment.

Foul Fact

Socrates died by drinking hemlock tea – which paralysed him before he gasped to breathe in a painful gurgling death.

Isaac Newton (1643–1727) was one of the most important scientists in history and is known as the 'father of modern science'. However, it took him a while to become a genius as he was born 11 to 15 weeks early. His mother said he could fit in a quart-sized cup when he was born.

Ouch! So that's why I'm called 'Eyes-ache' Newton.

Isaac didn't do particularly well in school and when put in charge of running the family farm, he failed so badly that an uncle took charge and sent him off to Cambridge University where he finally blossomed into a genius scholar. Sir Isaac Newton discovered the principle of gravity and defined force in his laws of motion, as well as inventing the cat flap in his spare time. Despite all his genius (and praise from cats), he was sometimes a bit odd. After his death, Newton's hair was examined and found to contain high levels of mercury from all his experiments. This might have caused some of his eccentric behaviour in later life.

Foul Fact

Newton stuck a needle in his eye to find out what went on inside his eye-socket. He poked it up between his eyelid and eye, twiddled it around and even dug around the back of his eyeball. He probably found out that it hurt!

Charles Darwin (1809–1882) was a

brilliant biologist, but when he was a boy he didn't do very well at school. He gave up his plan to become a doctor (partly because he hated the sight of blood), and was often told off by his father for being lazy and too dreamy. Charles later wrote, 'I was considered by all my masters and my father, a very ordinary boy, rather below the common standard of intellect.' Even so, Darwin went on to great things through hard work and real ability. Today he is famous for his important scientific studies and big ideas about evolution, which changed the way people think about the world.

Darwin taught-us so much!

Foul Fact

Darwin had a strange stomach for weird food. He ate such things as owls, hawks and bitterns at a club he belonged to where members munched away on wild creatures. When he was studying wildlife on Galapagos, Darwin rode giant tortoises and drank fluid from their bladders, which he described as having 'only a very slightly bitter taste.' Even so, it might be best to stick to fruit juice (but NOT hemlock tea).

Albert Einstein (1879–1955) worked on some of the most important discoveries and theories in all of science. Many consider him to be one of the super geniuses of the 20th century. His Theory of Relativity changed the way scientists look at the physical world: $E=mc^2$. (E is energy, m represents units of mass, and c is the speed of light).

But little Albert didn't show much promise as a boy. He didn't speak until he was four and didn't read until he was seven, causing his teachers and parents to think he had learning difficulties. He was even expelled from school and failed to get into university at first. He made it in the end, winning the Nobel Prize and changing the face of modern physics. Even so, Einstein was famous for having a bad memory as he couldn't remember names or dates. He also had some weird habits…

Foul facts

1 Einstein was known to do things like randomly pick grasshoppers up off the ground and eat them just to freak out his friends.

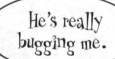

He's really bugging me.

These taste delicious!

3 When Einstein died, the pathologist at the hospital stole his brain and sliced it up to pickle it in jars. He also removed Einstein's eyeballs and they remain to this day in a safe deposit box in New York City.

2 Those close to the eccentric genius worried about his personal hygiene. He didn't clean himself regularly and often got so busy with his work that he began to smell revolting. Close friends would practically have to drag him into a shower to make him presentable, but Einstein himself never saw the need.

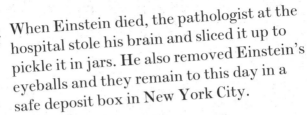

Maybe $E=mc^2$ also meant: Einstein = manky clothes^2

GENIUS
Einstein jokes

Einstein was travelling on a train when the conductor came down the aisle, checking the tickets. Einstein reached in his jacket but couldn't find his ticket, so he reached in his trouser pockets. It wasn't there, so he looked in his briefcase but couldn't find it. Then he looked in the seat beside him. He still couldn't find it.

The conductor said, 'Dr. Einstein, I know who you are. We all know who you are. I'm sure you bought a ticket. Don't worry about it.'

Einstein nodded and the conductor continued down the aisle. As he was ready to move to the next carriage, he turned around and saw the great physicist down on his hands and knees looking under his seat for his ticket.

The conductor rushed back and said, 'Dr. Einstein, Dr. Einstein, don't worry, I know who you are. No problem. You don't need a ticket. I'm sure you bought one.' Einstein looked at him and stuttered, 'Young man, I also know who I am. What I don't know is where I'm going.'

If only it were true

When Albert Einstein had to travel to give lectures, he was often keen to get back to his laboratory work. One night, as they were driving to yet another lecture, Einstein mentioned to his chauffeur (who happened to resemble Albert) that he was tired of making speeches.

'I have an idea, boss,' his chauffeur said. 'I've heard you give this speech so many times. I'll bet I could give it for you.' Einstein laughed loudly and said, 'Why not? Let's do it.'

When they arrived at the lecture hall, Einstein wore the chauffeur's cap and jacket and sat at the back for a rest. The chauffeur gave a great version of Einstein's speech and even answered a few questions expertly.

Suddenly a pompous professor stood up to ask an extremely difficult question about anti-matter formation, going on and on to make sure everyone in the audience knew that he was also a genius. Calmly the chauffeur fixed the professor with a steely stare and said, 'Sir, I am surprised that someone like you has asked such a simple question. To prove how basic it is, I will sit down and let my chauffeur at the back answer it.'

Girls are science geniuses, too!

Although many of the famous scientists in history were men (because few women got the chance to study), there have been some great female geniuses whose work changed the world of science.

Ada Lovelace (1815–1852) was a British mathematician who was the first real computer programmer in the world. Her father was Lord Byron (a famous poet who some saw as a genius, too) and her mother was a scientist who encouraged the young Ada in studying science. Ada later worked with the great Charles Babbage ('The father of computers') at the University of London on plans for an 'analytic engine'. She developed the first programming machines using mathematical algorithms. Such was her genius that the programming language, developed by the US Department of Defense, is named after her.

Marie Curie (1867–1934)

When it comes to clever women scientists, few names can match that of Marie Curie, the Polish scientist who became the first woman to win the Nobel Prize twice – in physics in 1903, then chemistry eight years later. With her husband, Pierre, she discovered the dangerous elements polonium and radium. The radiation she was exposed to in her work led to her death from leukaemia at the age of 66. Today a charity caring for terminally ill people bears her name.

Maria Goeppert-Mayer (1906–1972)

was a German-born American scientist and one of the most important figures in nuclear physics. She was exceptionally good at maths at school and she must have been super-clever because she passed the university entrance exam a year early, at the age of 17. Her development of atomic energy eventually led to Maria becoming the second woman, after Marie Curie, to win the Nobel Prize in Physics – in 1963. In fact, the great Albert Einstein once called her the 'German Marie Curie.' You don't get much more genius than that!

Now to the

BIG

question. Could YOU be a genius, too?

Puzzle time for geniuses

If you get all five of these riddles correct, you're on your way to becoming a real live genius. There again, you might be one already and get them all wrong!

Question 1: I am the beginning of everything, and the end of time and space. I am essential to creation, and I surround every place. What am I?
Answer: The letter 'e'

Question 2: The person who invented it doesn't want it. The person who bought it doesn't need it. The person who needs it doesn't know it. What is it?
Answer: A coffin

Question 3: How can you drop a raw egg from a height onto a concrete floor without cracking it?
Answer: Easy – concrete floors are very hard to crack!

Question 4: What part of a turkey has the most feathers?
Answer: The outside

Question 5: The more it dries, the wetter it gets. What is it?
Answer: A towel.

My brain has been teased to shreds.

We need more geniuses! So said Robert Streeter and Robert Hoehn, two American intelligence experts in the 1930s. Their brain-teasers were meant to test who might be a genius. Try these to discover if YOU are a top-class genius... or not!

1 Rearrange the following letters to make the name of a living creature:

B R I N O

2 What one word means both 'dodge' and 'immerse'?

3 When seen in a mirror, which of the following words printed in capital letters will look the same as when viewed directly?

MAN TOOT DEED

4 A man lived in a house that could be entered by only one door and five windows. Making certain that there was no one in the house one day, he went out for the afternoon. On his return, although the windows were still locked and unbroken and the door had not been forced, he discovered a thief in his house. If the thief did not use a skeleton key, or pick any of the locks, how did he get into the house?

In the following word, eliminate the second letter and every alternate letter thereafter. What word do the remaining letters form?

GLEAM

Rearrange the following letters so that they make the name of an article of furniture:

C H O C U

My father is the brother of your sister. What relative am I of yours? Cousin, nephew, son, uncle, son-in-law?

8

By eliminating one letter in each of four words in the following sentence, a new sentence of an entirely different meaning will remain. What is it?

They heard meat was stewed.

9

Which two of the following words are composed of the same letters?

AGATE, AGITATE, GATES, STAGS, STAGE, GRATE

There were three horses running in a race. Their names were Tally-ho, Sonny Boy, and Juanita.

Their owners were Mr Lewis, Mr Bailey and Mr Smith, although not necessarily in that order. Tally-ho unfortunately broke its ankle at the start of the race. Mr Smith owned a brown and white three-year old. Sonny Boy had previous winnings of £20,000. Mr Bailey lost heavily although his horse almost won. The horse that won was black. This race was the first race that the horse owned by Mr Lewis had run. What was the name of the horse that won?

Answers

1 ROBIN

2 DUCK

3 TOOT

4 The burglar entered through the door which the man had left unlocked!

5 GEM

6 COUCH

7 Nephew

8 The hard mat was sewed

9 GATES & STAGE

10 Get ready – hold on to your hats for a quick explanation: Mr Smith's horse couldn't be the winner because the horse that won was black. Mr Bailey's horse didn't win, so the owner of the winning horse must be Mr Lewis. Tally-ho couldn't have belonged to Mr Lewis as it fell at the start and broke its ankle. Sonny Boy couldn't have belonged to Mr Lewis because it had previously run. So, Juanita must have belonged to Mr Lewis and was the winner. (If you got that right, you must either be a genius or a keen gambler at the races!)

Another Conundrum to test your brain power

A cow conundrum coming up...

This might put you in a bad mooood.

A farmer died leaving his 19 cows to his three sons. When his sons opened the will, it read:

My eldest son should get 1/2 (half) of the total cows;

My middle son should be given 1/4 (quarter) of the total cows;

My youngest son should be given 1/5 (fifth) of the total cows.

As it's impossible to divide 19 into halves, quarters or fifths, the three sons started to fight with each other. One of them insisted on cutting some of the cows in half to make things easier to work out.

'That's stupid,' the eldest son said, 'why don't we ask the old woman in the cottage? She's meant to be a genius.'

So, they decided to go to the woman who was known to be very wise. She read the will patiently and, after giving due thought, she took them out to her backyard where a cow stood munching hay. 'You can have my cow as well. Now you'll have twenty cows to share among you all.' She divided the twenty cows according to their father's will.

Half of 20 = 10. So she gave the eldest son 10 cows.
Quarter of 20 = 5. So she gave the middle son 5 cows.
1/5 of 20 = 4. So she gave the youngest son 4 cows.

They added up how many cows they now had between them:
ELDEST SON.......10
MIDDLE SON......5
YOUNGEST SON...4
TOTAL IS......19.

This left one cow over, so the wise old lady said she would take her own cow back again. Problem solved!

So – it seems the key to being a genius is to believe that there is always a solution to a problem. After all, if we think that there is no solution, we won't be able to solve anything!

Don't worry if you got it wrong – just moooove on.

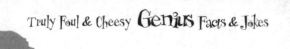

Leonardo Da Vinci

Leonardo Da Vinci (1452–1519) was not just an Italian painter and artist, he was also an engineer, sculptor, draftsman, inventor, scientist, mathematician, costume maker, writer and musician. Yes, he was exceptionally gifted in so many areas and maybe the most talented person on the planet ever – an amazing polymath (a polymath is not a parrot that can count, but someone with a wide range of skills and knowledge).

Leonardo produced so much, even though he left many of his paintings and inventions unfinished. He was both ambidextrous and dyslexic, which enabled him to draw with one hand while writing backwards with the other. He often wrote backwards, simply to make his work difficult to read. His famous paintings of the Mona Lisa and The Last Supper are worth a fortune today.

Foul Fact

Have you got no body else to play with?

One of Leonardo's jobs was to cut up human corpses at the hospital in Florence. He not only cut them up but drew them to learn all about the human body.

Of course, we all know that teachers and professors must be geniuses. Maybe not all, according to these jokes...

Teacher: Whoever answers my next question correctly must be a genius and can go home immediately.

A boy throws his bag out the window.

Teacher: Who just threw that?

Boy: Me! I'm going home now.

In class one day, the teacher asked Johnny over to her desk after a test, and said, 'Johnny, I have a feeling that you have been cheating on your tests.' Johnny was astounded and insisted there was no proof and besides, he was a genius.

'Well,' said the teacher, 'I was looking over your test and the question was, 'Who was the first American President?', and Mary who sits next to you, put 'George Washington,' and so did you.'

'So, everyone knows that he was the first president,' Johnny insisted.

'Well, just wait a minute,' said the teacher. 'The next question was, 'Who freed the slaves?' Mary put Abraham Lincoln and so did you.'

'Well, I read the history book last night and I remembered that,' said Johnny.

'Wait, wait,' said the teacher. 'The next question was, 'Who was the next president after George Washington?' Mary put 'I don't know,' and you put, 'Me neither'.'

Teacher: If a lion is chasing you, what would you do?

Christy: I'd climb a tree.

Teacher: And if the lion climbs a tree?

Christy: I'd jump in the lake and swim.

Teacher: And if the lion also jumps in the water and swims after you?

Christy: Hey, are you on my side or on the lion's?

Off to university?

A university professor is so cross with all the poor work handed in by his students that he stands in front of the class and asks if anyone in the class is an idiot – and if there is one, then he or she should stand up. After a minute a student stands up, so the professor asks, 'So you admit to being an idiot, do you?'
The boy replies, 'No, I just didn't want to see you standing there all by yourself.'

These jokes are for intellectuals.

Four university students weren't too worried about their final exams coming up. In fact, they felt so confident that they decided to drive down to the beach together for the weekend. They had a great time but after so much partying, they slept all day Sunday and didn't make it back to college until Monday – missing their final exam. They decided to find their professor and explain why they'd missed it – telling a giant lie. They told him they'd gone away to do scientific research over the weekend but got a flat tyre on the way back, didn't have a spare and couldn't get help for a long time. As a result, they'd only just got back.

The professor thought it over and then agreed they could make up their final exam the following day. The students were relieved they'd got away with it and studied hard that night – all night – and went in the next day at the time the professor had told them. He placed them in separate rooms and handed each of them a test booklet, (which was out of 100 points) and told them to begin. The first problem was worth five points and really easy. They all thought in their separate rooms, 'this is going to be so easy'.

Each student then turned the page. Question 2 (for 95 points): Which tyre?

Loopy limericks

An eccentric young genius at school
Thought he was being so cool
By drinking pure starch
On the last day of March...
But woke up a complete April Fool
(set rigid!)

If I put a tube of Smarties in my trouser pocket, does that make me a Smartie Pants?

Most geniuses seem rather quirky,
Hyperactive and terribly perky.
Their energies are
Extremely bizarre,
As they flap about like a mad turkey.

Warning: this limerick
contains nuts (and a nutcase)

A professor of chestnuts and conkers
Gave lectures on nuts – they
were stonkers!
Crowds flocked just to see
He was out of his tree...
A genius – but totally bonkers.

Eccentric geniuses

Some very clever people have been more famous for their quirkiness than their genius. Sometimes the price to pay for being a clever-clogs is becoming a bit of an oddball.

How time FLIES during dinner

William Buckland (1784–1856) is famous for two things: he was the first geologist to write a full account of a fossil dinosaur, and he was incredibly eccentric when it came to animals and food. His love of natural history resulted in him turning his house into a zoo. He didn't just fill his rooms with animals of every kind, he often ate them – and served them to guests. He claimed to have eaten his way through every animal around. The creatures that he said tasted worst were bluebottle flies and moles. Now there's a surprise!

FOUL ALERT...

Buckland often served his dinner guests panther, crocodile and mouse. As if that wasn't weird enough, he once got hold of a relic in a silver casket – the heart of the French King, Louis XIV. Yes, you've guessed – he munched the lot. How foul is that?

Hetty Green (1834–1916) was a genius American businesswoman with a gift for making huge amounts of money, becoming the richest woman in the world. Mind you, a lot of her wealth came from being an eccentric miser, known as the 'Witch of Wall Street'. To save even more money, Hetty would work out of trunks at her local bank so she wouldn't have to pay rent for an office. When her son fell ill, she disguised herself and took him to a charity hospital, but when they realised who she was, she fled claiming she would cure her son herself. Unfortunately, he got gangrene and had to have his leg amputated.

FOUL ALERT...

Hetty always wore the same black dress and never changed her underwear until it wore out. No wonder Hetty was STINKING rich.

William Archibald Spooner

(1844 –1930) was a famous professor at Oxford University. Although he was very clever, he was always getting his words in a muddle (or murds in a wuddle). In fact, this accidental swapping of letters and sounds in a sentence became known as a 'spoonerism', named after him.

One example of his mistakes includes 'Go and shake a tower' (meaning 'go and take a shower'). Students rushed to Professor Spooner's lectures just to hear him make mistakes!

'The bog darked and the RAT can away'. Work that out!

Some famous spoonerisms are:

'Let us glaze our asses to the queer old Dean'
(...raise our glasses to the dear old Queen)

'We'll have the hags flung out'
(...flags hung out)

Foul alert...

To a lazy student, he said 'You have tasted a whole worm' (wasted a whole term).

Oscar Wilde (1854–1900) was a very gifted writer, witty speaker and playwright. He often annoyed people by telling them what a genius he was! He also upset people by his weird clothes and outrageous comments. While studying at Oxford University, Oscar would walk through the streets with a lobster on a lead. His room was decorated with bright blue china, sunflowers and peacock feathers. He became a real Victorian celebrity and once, when going through customs in America, he apparently said in a loud voice: 'I have nothing to declare except my genius'.

Treating me like this is so shellfish.

'F' ALERT...

Just try saying Oscar's full name three times fast: Oscar Fingal O'Flahertie Wills Wilde.

His last words were 'My wallpaper and I are fighting a duel to the death. One or other of us has got to go.'
The wallpaper won.

NOT so genius jokes

A man in a hot air balloon was lost so he descended to ask a woman in a field below where he was heading.

'Can you help me?' he called down to her. 'I promised a very important person I would meet him an hour ago, but even though I'm a genius, I'm not sure where I am.'

The woman below replied, 'You're in a hot air balloon, about ten metres above the ground. You are between 40 and 41 degrees north and almost 60 degrees west.'

'Bah, you must be an engineer,' the balloonist scoffed.

'That's right,' the woman answered. 'How can you tell?'

'Because everything you've told me,' the balloonist sneered, 'is technically correct but I've got no idea what to make of your information and the fact is, I'm still lost. Frankly, you haven't helped me in the slightest and you've now delayed my progress and made matters worse.'

The woman smiled. 'You must be a politician.'

'Yes, I am. I'm a very important person and a genius at running the country.'

I'm not a basket case but a high-minded genius!

'I thought you must be a politician,' she went on. 'After all, you don't know where you are or where you're going. You have risen to your position due to a lot of hot air. You made a promise which you've no idea how to keep and you expect people beneath you to solve your problems for you. The fact is, you are in exactly the same position as you were before we met – but somehow it's now suddenly all my fault. Unlike you, I've always kept my feet firmly on the ground and know exactly what I'm doing, without needing to have my head in the clouds. After all, common sense can be so much more useful than genius!'

Another hot air balloon was flying high over the mountains when it was struck by lightning. The four people in the basket were terrified at the sound of air hissing from the balloon above them. The pilot looked at the gas cylinder and announced they were out of gas and the balloon would drop like a stone any minute. Luckily there were three parachutes – so he grabbed one and jumped from the basket. But that left only two parachutes and three people: a professor, an old lady and a young hiker.

Suddenly the professor grabbed for a parachute, strapped it on his bag and announced, 'As I am a world-famous professor, a genius of mathematics and the cleverest man on the planet, it is my duty to live and preserve my genius.' He leapt from the basket, leaving the two passengers staring down to the rocks miles below.

The little old lady grasped the young hiker's hand.

'You take the last parachute. You're young and fit, with your life before you. I'm just a simple old woman and I've had a good life...'

The hiker grinned and passed her a parachute and said, 'No need to worry. We've got a parachute each. That professor genius who's the cleverest guy on the planet just jumped out with my backpack.'

Animal antics of pure genius

SUPERDOG

A butcher sees a dog sitting outside his shop so goes out to shoo it away. As he shouts at it to 'go away', the butcher sees £20 and a note in its mouth, reading '8 lamb chops please'. Amazed, the butcher takes the money, puts a bag of chops in the dog's mouth and quickly closes the shop.

He follows the dog and watches it wait for a green light at the crossing, look both ways and trot across the road to a bus stop. The dog then checks the timetable and sits on the bench.

When a bus arrives, it walks round to the front, looks at the number, then boards the bus.

It's well known dogs are intelligent. I read it in a book.

The butcher follows in complete amazement. As the bus travels out of the town and into the countryside, the dog stands on its back legs, reaches up with its front paw and pushes the 'stop' bell and gets off. The butcher follows.

The dog runs up to a house, drops its bag on the step and barks repeatedly. No one answers so it goes back down the path, takes a big run and throws itself against the door.

Thwack!

It does this over and over again. Still no answer.

Now the dog jumps on a wall, walks around the garden, barks repeatedly at the window, jumps off and waits at the front door. Eventually an old man opens it and starts cursing and shouting at the dog.

The butcher runs up screaming at the man. 'What are you doing? Stop screaming at that dog. It's a genius!'

The old man guffaws scathingly. 'Ha – genius, my foot. It's the second time this week that stupid dog's forgotten its key!'

CAT GENIUS

We cats are never out of eduCATion.

A vet is driving through town when he sees a sign in front of a house: 'Singing Cat for Sale.'

'This I must hear,' he laughs to himself. He rings the doorbell and the owner tells him the cat is in the back garden. The vet finds a ginger tom sitting under a tree.

'Do you really sing?' he asks.

'Yep,' the cat replies. 'If you pay me.'

The vet is astonished. 'You can talk brilliantly! Tell me about yourself.'

The cat looks up with a sigh and says, 'Well, I discovered that I could sing when I was very young – no more than a kitten, really. It's just a natural gift I have. Some call me a feline genius. I can even speak French and Russian but I prefer to sing in Italian. I sang in all the great opera houses before settling down with a talented soprano. She was a gorgeous tabby and we got married. Sadly, after having lots of prize-winning kittens, she ran off with a long-haired Siamese in the chorus. Now I'm divorced, retired and apparently for sale.'

You're looking very pail.

The vet is speechless. He rushes indoors to ask the owner how much he wants for the cat.

'Ten pounds.'

'Ten pounds? I'd pay far more than that for a talking parrot. That cat is a total genius. Why on earth are you selling him so cheaply?'

'Because he's nothing but a liar. He never did any of that stuff. He's just a con artist with the power of purr-suasion and a bad cat-itude. And as for all that stuff about being an opera singer, don't believe a word of it. He's only in a cats' chorus in that mew-sical 'Cats'. He can't reach the low notes – so that's why he's going for a song, as he's only a tenor.'

Feel free to groan out loud!

And finally...

Here's a slice of genius pie (not cheesy pie but Pi, as in the ratio of a circle's circumference to its diameter, which is equal to 3.14159265358979323846... the digits go on forever without repeating).

In the Guinness Book of World Records, you can find how a man memorised 70,000 numbers accurately (the decimal places of Pi, if you're interested). This feat of genius was achieved by Rajveer Meena in Vellore, India, in 2015. Rajveer wore a blindfold throughout the entire recall, which took nearly 10 hours.

So, if you've got a good memory for numbers and you're something of a whiz-kid, how about trying to memorise something amazing? Maybe the whole of this book!

[If you think that challenge is batty but if you survived some of the truly foul facts and cheesy jokes in this book, take a look at the other mad titles in this revolting series. They're all guaranteed to make you groan and squirm like never before. You have been warned!]

QUIZ

1. What was the name of the room in medieval castles where nobles could use the toilet?

a) Garden

b) Garderobe

c) Gallery

2. Which of these did Thomas Edison invent?

a) Telegraph

b) Telephone

c) Television

3. What animal did Nikola Tesla love?

a) Budgerigars

b) Pigeons

c) Turtles

I may be slow but now I'm a shellebrity.

4. What fibre is used to make bulletproof vests?

a) Teflon

b) Wool

c) Kevlar

5. What did Marie Van Britten Brown invent?

a) 3D TV

b) HD TV

c) CCTV

6. What was found in Isaac Newton's hair after his death?

a) Mercury

b) Shampoo

c) Hair gel

7. What was Leonardo da Vinci?

a) A polygon

b) A polymath

c) A politician

8. What elements did Marie Curie discover?

a) Polonium and radium

b) Helium and nitrogen

c) Barium and magnesium

9. Who was the world's first computer programmer?

a) Bill Gates

b) Thomas Edison

c) Ada Lovelace

10. Who killed himself by drinking hemlock?

a) Socrates

b) Aristotle

c) Julius Caesar

How many did you guess right?

Answers:

1 = b
2 = a
3 = b
4 = c
5 = c
6 = a
7 = b
8 = a
9 = c
10 = a

GLOSSARY

Algorithm: a set of rules that can be used to solve mathematical problems in calculation.

Calculator: devices used to aid someone in making mathematical calculations.

Commode: an item of furniture with a chamber pot hidden inside it.

Fluorescent lighting: light produced by passing an electrical current through mercury vapour.

Hemlock: a very poisonous plant with a purple-spotted stem and white flowers that grows in Europe.

Laxative: a type of medicine used to stimulate a bowel movement and cure constipation.

Moat: a ditch filled with water surrounding a castle, used to defend it from attack.

Sanitation: the practice of maintaining a hygienic environment by removing waste products such as sewage.

INDEX

I finished reading this Truly
Foul & Cheesy book on:

........../........../..........